CAPTAIN MORONI'S
TITLE OF LIBERTY

To Anissa, with much love
Sherrie Johnson

To Bob and Kathie Wilson, for your enthusiasm and support
Tyler Lybbert

© 1994 Deseret Book Company

All rights reserved. No part of this book may be reproduced in any form or by any means without permission in writing from the publisher, Deseret Book Company, P.O. Box 30178, Salt Lake City, Utah 84130. This work is not an official publication of The Church of Jesus Christ of Latter-day Saints. The views expressed herein are the responsibility of the author and do not necessarily represent the position of the Church or of Deseret Book Company.

Deseret Book is a registered trademark of Deseret Book Company.

Printed in Mexico.

10 9 8 7 6 5 4 3 2

ISBN 0-87579-813-6

Designed by Craig Geertsen.

CAPTAIN MORONI'S
TITLE OF LIBERTY

WRITTEN BY
SHERRIE JOHNSON

ILLUSTRATED BY
TYLER LYBBERT

DESERET BOOK COMPANY
SALT LAKE CITY, UTAH

"If you will make me king," Amalickiah said, tempting the judges of the Nephites, "I will make you rulers over the people."

Flattered by his wicked words, some of the lower judges joined Amalickiah. Together they made plans to take away the liberty of the people, to overthrow the church, and to make him king.

You say it, A-mahl-a-KI-ah.

Moroni, the chief commander of the armies of the Nephites, heard what Amalickiah was doing and rent his cloak. Taking a piece of the torn fabric, he wrote upon it, "In memory of our God, our religion, and freedom, and our peace, our wives, and our children." Then he fastened the piece of cloak to a pole.

Next, Moroni put on his head-plate and breastplate. He girded his armor about his loins and took up his shield.

"Gird" means to fasten around you.

Holding the flag, which he called the Title of Liberty, Moroni bowed himself to the earth and prayed mightily. He asked God for the blessings of liberty to be upon his people.

When he had poured out his soul to God, Moroni named all the land, both on the north and on the south, a chosen land and the land of liberty.

"Surely God shall not suffer that we who are Christians shall be trodden down and destroyed, unless we bring it upon ourselves because of our sins," he said.

After he had said these words, Moroni went forth among the people, waving the Title of Liberty so that all might see the writing. "Whosoever will maintain this title upon the land," he cried, "let them come forth in the strength of the Lord, and enter into a covenant that they will maintain their rights, and their religion, that the Lord God may bless them."

From everywhere, the people came running with their armor girded about their loins.

When they reached Moroni, they rent their clothing and threw the rent garments at Moroni's feet. "We covenant with our God," they said, "that we shall be destroyed if we shall fall into transgression. Yea, the Lord may cast us at the feet of our enemies, even as we have cast our garments at Moroni's feet, if we shall fall into transgression."

Moroni answered, "Let us preserve our liberty!"

"Transgression" is another word for sin.

Then Moroni reminded them of their ancestor, Joseph, who was sold into Egypt. Joseph's coat had been rent by his brothers, covered with blood, and taken to their father, Jacob. When Jacob saw the coat, he thought Joseph was dead, and he prophesied that a remnant of his people would be preserved, just as a remnant of Joseph's coat had been preserved. Jacob also said that part of the people would perish, just as part of the coat had perished.

When a piece of cloth is all that's left of a bigger piece, it is called a remnant.

"Perhaps the people of Joseph who will perish as his garment perished are these men who have chosen evil," Moroni said. "But we might also perish if we do not stand fast in the faith of Christ."

After Moroni said these words, he went forth to other parts of the land where there were dissensions and gathered all the people who desired to maintain their liberty.

What are dissensions?

They're angry quarrels between people.

When Amalickiah saw how many people followed Moroni, he began to worry. He grew so frightened that he took his band and fled from the land.

But Moroni did not want Amalickiah to join with the Lamanites and make war. With his army, he followed Amalickiah into the wilderness. There they caught Amalickiah's band and captured most of them. However, Amalickiah and a few others escaped.

Moroni marched the prisoners back to the land of Zarahemla. Many of the prisoners repented and entered into a covenant to support the cause of freedom. They were allowed to go free. The few who refused to make a covenant to support liberty were put to death so they could make no more war.

To celebrate, the people put Titles of Liberty upon all the towers throughout the land of the Nephites. Every time they looked at them, they remembered Moroni's words that if they always followed God, they would live in peace.

This story is in Alma, chapter forty-six.